First published in Australia 2020
By Justine Sless
Copyright ©Justine Sless 2020
The moral right of the author has been asserted.
Justine Sless has asserted her right under the Copyright, Designs and Patents Act 1988, to be identified as author of this book.
All rights reserved. No part of this book may be reproduced or transmitted in any form or by any means, electronic or mechanical, including photocopying, recording or any information storage or retrieval system, without prior permission in writing from the publisher.

ISBN: 978-0-646-81745-3 (paperback)
Cover and internal design by Curtis Miller.
Editor Emma Cayley.

For Jess and Ruby

Introduction

These are some of my favourite recipes for you to savour. They come from years working as a chef, time spent at the kitchen bench raising my kids, and meals shared with family and friends for Jewish holidays like Rosh Hashana and Passover.

The illustrations are by my eldest daughter, Ruby, who has been magically creating a whole host of quirky characters ever since she was very little.

For each recipe, I've suggested music and drinks as extra ingredients, if you will.

This recipe book has been on the boil for a while, but I present it to you now in the midst of the coronavirus pandemic. I hope that the aromas and tastes provide comfort and sanctuary until we can all fress* on a sumptuous meal with loved ones, gathered together from near and far to eat, drink, dance and be merry.

*Fress is the Yiddish word meaning to eat or nosh often or in large quantities.

Many of the recipes were originally made for Jewish celebrations – but can be eaten any time of the year.

Please note the recipes do not comply with Kosher guidelines.

Ingredients use Australian Standard measuring cups and spoons.

Contents

Flavoursome

Seared Salmon Salad 8
Damn Fine Fish Cakes 11
Rosh Hashana Lamb 12
Winter Lamb 14
Shakshuka 16
Eggplant Jam 18

Sweet as

Best Brownie -Right On, Right On 22
Fruit Cake 25
Fruity Peppercorn Cake 27
Pear, Fig and Honey Cake 28
Raspberry, Chocolate and Sour Cream Cake 31
Matzoh Crack 32
Sticky Date Pudding 35

Flavoursome

Seared Salmon Salad

The trick with this recipe is to sear the salmon so that it stays firm and a little bit undercooked on the inside. And don't over-marinade the fish - a couple of hours is the most it will need.

Ingredients

700g of salmon - a middle piece (the tail piece is not thick enough)
Splash of sesame oil for cooking

Marinade

⅓ cup sweet soy sauce (kecap manis)
1 tsp sesame oil
1 tsp crushed ginger
4 kaffir lime leaves, very thinly sliced and diced
Juice and zest of 1 lime
Dash fish sauce

Salad

(These ingredients can be purchased from a Vietnamese grocery store)
2 handfuls snow pea flower shoots
200g snow peas, topped, tailed and finely sliced
½ cucumber, de-seeded and cut into thin strips
2 carrots, peeled and sliced with a julienne peeler or cut by hand
250g bag fresh bean shoots
2 tbsp fried shallots

Salad Dressing

Juice and zest of 1 lime
4 tbsp of kecap manis
½ tsp sesame oil
Put in a lidded jar and shake it, baby

Method

Marinade

Mix ingredients in a small bowl and heat for 40 seconds in microwave or on a stove top till warm before adding to salmon.

Salmon

Use fish tweezers to remove bones from salmon.
Skin the fish(Google if you don't know how).
Cut the salmon into good-sized chunks - about 2.5cm (no smaller or it will break apart when cooked).
Put salmon into a bowl and pour the marinade over it, making sure all chunks are coated.
Marinade for no more than two hours.
Heat a splash of sesame oil in non-stick frying pan – make sure it's very hot before adding the salmon.
Fry the salmon – in batches if needed.
Don't add excess marinade when frying.
The salmon needs to sear so that it darkens and gets a little crispy. This will happen quickly, so watch it, but don't fuss with it or it will break apart.
With tongs, turn the salmon once during the frying process.
Set the salmon aside.
On a large, preferably round platter, place the washed snow pea shoot flowers around the edge of the plate, like a garland.
Layer the salad ingredients, starting with the bean shoots, then carrots, then snow peas and create a mound so that there's some height to the salad.
Pour the salad dressing over the salad.
Place the seared salmon pieces around the salad
Sprinkle deep-fried shallots over the salad.
This can be served cold but tastes best if the salmon is still warm.

Play Nina Simone's "Feeling Fine" and drink with iced tea or a Monteith's pale ale.

Damn Fine Fish Cakes

These Damn Fine Fish Cakes are a little disco in your mouth and are a far cry from the fish cakes I had growing up (in Sunderland, in the north east of England) - made with cod, potato and breadcrumbs.

Ingredients

500g white fish - flathead fillets work well
250g shelled prawns, chopped roughly into three pieces
6 kaffir lime leaves, chopped into julienne strips, then fine diced
1 tsp red curry paste
Handful of chopped fresh coriander
1 egg white
1 lime, cut into wedges
Sweet chilli sauce
Peanut oil for shallow frying,
 approx. ½ cup Iceberg lettuce for serving

Method

Chop fish into chunks.

Put fish, kaffir lime leaves (can purchase from Vietnamese grocery store), egg white, coriander and red curry paste into food processor until blended - it will look like a thick paste.

Remove and put in bowl, stir through prawns.

Heat oil in frying pan.

Use a bowl of cold water to wet hands.

Form walnut-sized balls of mixture - don't make them too neat.

Shallow fry on both sides until golden.

Remove and drain on kitchen towel.

Break lettuce into 'cups' - pieces big enough to wrap around fish cakes.

Place fish cakes at the side of the lettuce cups.

Serve with lime wedges and sweet chilli dipping sauce.

I also use crispy prawn chilli paste (I adore this paste - buy it from an Asian grocery store, you won't regret it!).

Serve with Asahi Super Dry beer or Bickford's grapefruit cordial, mineral water, ice, mint leaves and lime wedges and boogie to "Waiting for the Train" by Flash in the Pan.

Rosh Hashana Lamb

This dish is a balance of sweet, aromatic and rich flavours. Take your time preparing this dish, meditate on the year gone by and anticipate the joy of the new year to come.

Jewish New Year is marked by the blowing of the shofar and begins the ten days of penitence culminating in Yom Kippur.

Ingredients

Leg of lamb (2-3kg)
3 sweet potatoes, peeled and diced
250g of dried pitted dates, chopped
6 dried figs, chopped
1 onion, finely chopped
4 cloves of garlic, crushed
1 stick of cinnamon
3 star anise
3 tsp of dried cumin
4 tbsp of honey
1 jar of passata (400g)
1 cup beef stock or water
Big splash good olive oil
Box of cous cous (500g)
Knob of butter
¼ cup currants
¼ cup dry-fried pepitas
½ lemon - juice and rind finely chopped
Handful of chopped continental parsley

Method

To prepare lamb

Trim excess fat from lamb.

Heat oil in cast-iron pot and sear lamb so that it is brown on all sides.

Remove lamb and set aside.

Fry onion and garlic on low heat in pot with cumin, star anise and cinnamon stick. Add more oil if required.

Add dates, figs and honey. Stir with a wooden spoon so that the mixture doesn't stick to the pan.

Cook till fruits soften.

Add the lamb.

Add diced sweet potato, passata and stock or water.

Bring just to the boil then turn the heat down low.

Put the lid on the pot and cook on low heat for 6-8 hours.

Every hour or so, spoon the sauce over the lamb so that it doesn't dry out. Turn the lamb over every hour.

Before serving, take the meat off the bone and remove any excess fat.

Cut up (or tear apart) the larger pieces of meat and return the meat to the pot.

Prepare cous cous

Pour box of cous cous into a deep bowl, add knob of butter, pour boiling water over the cous cous so that it is just covered.

Put a plate over the bowl for about 5-10 minutes or until the cous cous is soft.

Stir in currants, pepitas, juice and rind of lemon, and handful of freshly chopped continental parsley.

Serve cous cous on the side with the Rosh Hashana Lamb.

Shana Tova - blow the shofar and eat this wonderous dish!

Serve with a good red wine.

Winter Lamb

Follow the ingredients list loosely, use up what you have in the fridge and pantry, replace fresh tomatoes for tinned, add more vegetables, and if you don't have any legumes, please don't worry, leave them out.

This can be made before you head out to work, which will mean you arrive home to a lovely cooked dinner. If you're working from home then prepare this in the morning and enjoy it at the end of the day.

Ingredients

½ leg of lamb, trim off excess fat
2 sweet potatoes, peeled and diced
2 carrots, diced
Half a head of celery, diced
1 tin of tomatoes (400g) or jar of passata (400g)
1 tin of pulses, chickpeas, lentils or borlotti beans (250g)
1 onion, diced

4 cloves garlic, peeled and crushed (crush cloves with a sprinkle of salt as it brings out the juices)
Zest and juice of 1 1emon
1 tbsp of chopped rosemary
1 cup water or beef stock
2 tsp ground cumin
1 tbsp of good Hungarian sweet paprika
Splash of good olive oil
Handful of freshly chopped parsley

Method

This recipe assumes ownership of a slow cooker. (If you don't have one then use a cast-iron pot with a lid on it.)

Sear the lamb on all sides in a frying pan with a splash of olive oil.

Put lamb into slow cooker.

Fry onions, garlic, cumin, sweet paprika, vegetables and rosemary with another splash of olive oil. Let the flavours sweat for five minutes or so.

Put vegetables in slow cooker.

De-glaze the pan with tomatoes so that all of juices from the seared meat and vegetables come away from the base.

Pour tomatoes onto meat and vegetables.

Rinse legumes and add to slow cooker.

Ensure that the lamb and veg are covered in stock or water.

Set the slow cooker to maximum cooking time.

When you're ready for dinner, crack open a good red wine or make a strong cup of tea.

Skim the excess fat from the sauce.

Take the lamb out of the slow cooker, remove any excess fat and take off the bone. Cut up or tear lamb from the bone and return to the slow cooker.

Remove any bones from the slow cooker and discard.

Sprinkle freshly chopped parsley and a squeeze of lemon onto dish before serving.

Serve with crusty bread, eat slowly and, if you're sharing the meal with loved ones, talk over the day you've had together.

"Tiny Dancer" by Elton John is a great song to accompany this dish. Red wine is a good accompaniment or, at the end of the meal, enjoy a fine single malt whiskey.

Shakshuka

This dish is a little bit Moroccan, a little bit Yemeni, a little bit Israeli and a whole lot of smoky loveliness. You can eat it for breakfast, lunch or dinner.

Ingredients

1 eggplant

½ pumpkin, de-seeded, peeled and diced (Kent pumpkin is best)

1 fresh tomato

1 tbsp tomato paste

4 eggs

1 tsp ground cumin

100g goats cheese

Cracked black pepper

2 tbsp fresh continental parsley, chopped

1 tbsp olive oil

Method

Place eggplant on open gas flame (or electric element) of stove top.

Turn the eggplant until it is charred all over.

Cool eggplant and peel off the skin.

Place eggplant flesh in a bowl.

Boil pumpkin till soft.

Roughly mash together eggplant, pumpkin, tomato paste, ground cumin, pepper and olive oil.

Place mixture in non-stick frying pan or cast-iron frying pan on low heat. Add chopped tomatoes on top.

Once mixture is hot, carefully break in eggs, one at a time, keeping them whole.

Place lid on pan till eggs are poached.

Serve with sprinkle of freshly chopped parsley.

Shakshuka can be cooked and served in individual mini cast-iron frying pans or ramekins and cooked in the oven.

Serve with a good sourdough, toasted and buttered, for breakfast, lunch or dinner.

Listen to "Bella Ciao di Risaia" by I Viaggiatori with Kavisha Mazzella and drink with strong tea or red wine.

Eggplant Jam

This luscious combination of roasted eggplant, lemon and sweet paprika can be served at Passover dinner instead of chopped liver. You can also spread this onto wraps, dollop it on top of salads or barbecued veg and meats.

Ingredients

3 eggplants
1 lemon juice and zest
4 cloves garlic
4-6 tbsp sweet paprika
1 tsp cumin
1 tsp brown sugar
6-12 tablespoons of vegetable oil
½ cup water
1 tbsp of chopped parsley
Matzoh to serve

Method

Cube eggplants then roast with garlic with 6-10 tbsp oil till soft and brown. (Leave the skin on the garlic).

In frying pan add 1 tbsp oil, cumin, sweet paprika and lemon zest and fry slowly for a few minutes.

Roughly mash eggplant and garlic with a fork and put mixture into the frying pan.

Stir in lemon juice and brown sugar.

Turn heat down low and put a lid on frying pan.

After 10 minutes or so, mash the eggplant again. The aim is to mash the white flesh into the paprika mix to give it a jam-like appearance.

Add water and simmer on low for around 30 minutes. The consistency should be very glossy and be a good red colour.

Serve warm and sprinkle with freshly chopped continental parsley. Break large pieces of matzoh around the bowl so that guests can serve themselves.

Store in airtight sterilised jar for up to two weeks in the fridge.

Serve with a good red wine (not Kosher wine!) and eat while playing The Barry Sisters "Passover Medley Dayenu".

Passover is a Jewish celebration commemorating the liberation of the Israelites from Egyptian slavery. The main event of this festival is the Passover dinner.

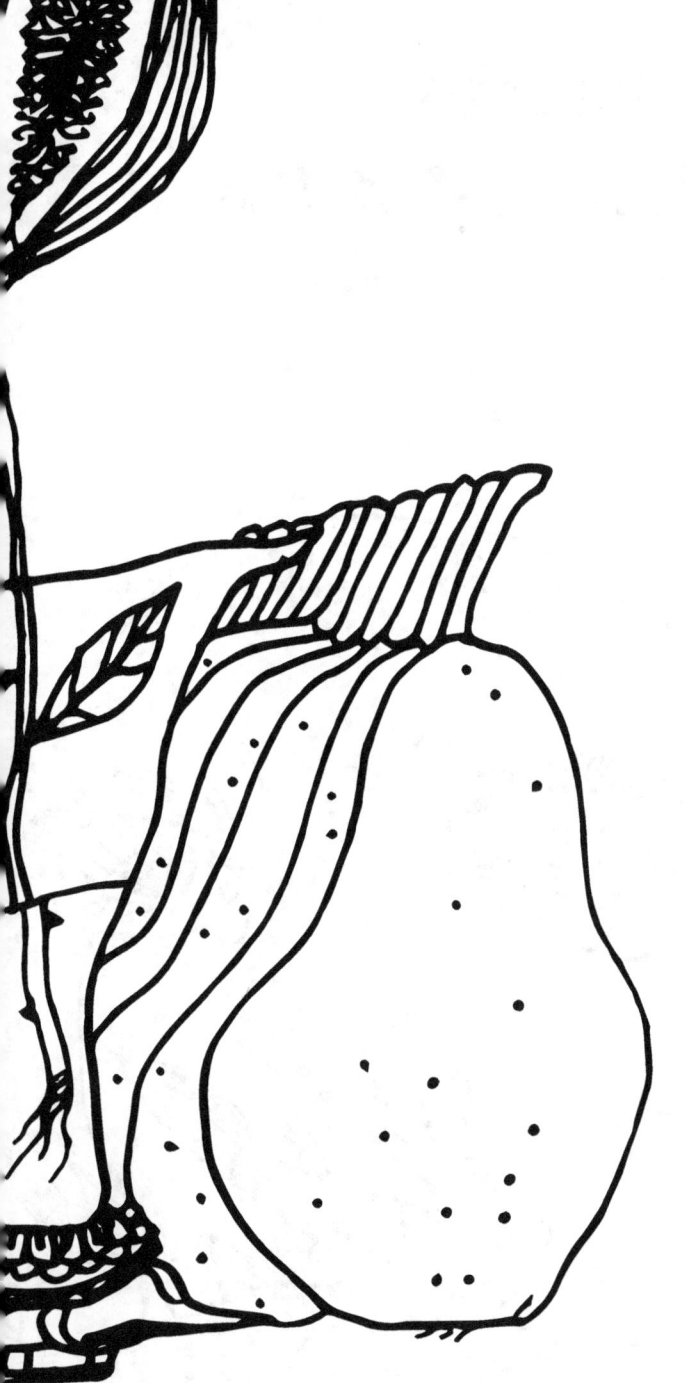

Sweet as

Best Brownie - Right On, Right On

It's the salt and the teaspoon of instant coffee that makes these brownies so good.

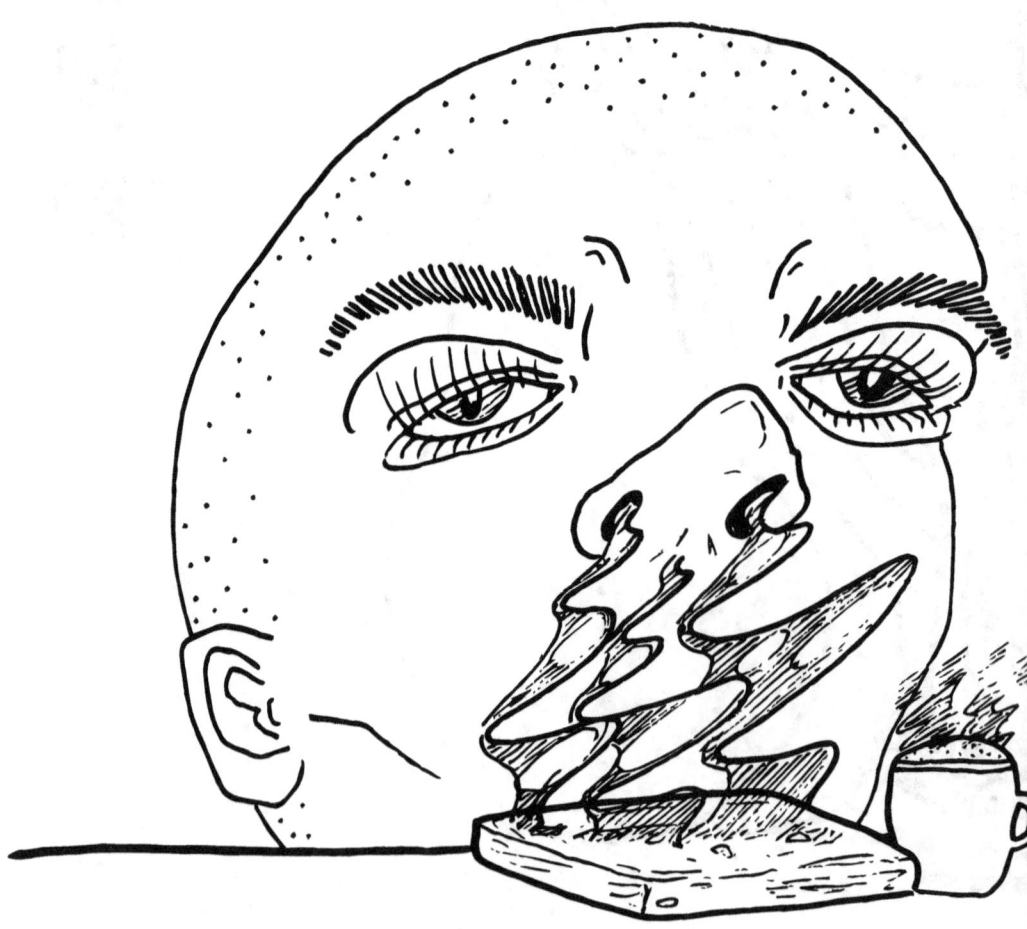

Ingredients

170g butter - salted and preferably Lurpak (don't use a home-brand butter - it just won't work. Trust me on this!)

200g dark chocolate (70% Lindt is good)

2 eggs

¾ cup caster sugar

⅓ cup plain flour

1 tsp instant coffee

Pinch salt (Maldon Sea Salt Flakes are the best)

200g white chocolate, chopped

Method

Pre-heat oven to 150°C.

Line 23cm square cake tin with baking paper.

Melt butter and dark chocolate together.

Lightly mix eggs, sugar, coffee (dissolved in 1 tbsp hot water) and salt.

Fold in the flour.

Stir in melted chocolate and butter until the mixture is shiny and smooth.

Fold in chopped white chocolate.

Pour mixture into tin.

Bake for 30 minutes at 150°C.

Cool in tin, then remove and wrap in baking paper and foil.

Refrigerate overnight.

Can be stored in airtight container in fridge for up to a week. (Or freeze for up to a month - can be frozen in smaller pieces and cut up as required).

Serve with good coffee or Yorkshire Tea.

Make, bake, dance and eat to "Get it On" by T Rex.

Fruit Cake

This is a really easy cake to make. You can play around with the ingredients to get the balance of flavours you enjoy.

This is a fab cake for vegans and those who love a Country Women's Association kind of a cake.

Ingredients

300g mixed fruit (I use 200g of currants, 50g cranberries, 50g mixed peel. You can use any mix you want - dried dates and figs (chopped into quarters) are also great).

2½ cups of liquid (I use earl grey tea. You can use fruit juice, which will produce a sweeter cake)

3 cups self-raising flour

1 tsp ground nutmeg

3 tsp ground cinnamon

⅓ cup of brown sugar - optional (but it does make the cake nice and rich)

Zest of one orange finely chopped

My friend Karen road-tested this recipe and suggests spelt flour instead of white self-raising flour, and a teaspoon of dried chilli to add depth of flavour.

Method

Place all fruits into a large mixing bowl.

Stir in liquid. I use strong hot earl grey tea, but this works just as well with cold liquid.

Cover overnight at room temperature.

Pre-heat oven to 150°C.

Line 23cm square tin (6cm deep) with baking paper.

Fold flour, cinnamon and nutmeg into fruit mix.

Stir well - ensure that all of the flour has been mixed in.

Bake on lowest shelf in oven for around 40-50 minutes or until skewer tests clean.

When cake is cool, remove from tin and store in airtight container for at least one day before slicing.

Serve with cheese - Wensleydale really is the only option - and a strong cup of tea.

"We'll Meet Again" by Vera Lynn is a good soundtrack to accompany the baking process. "Reasons to be Cheerful" by Ian Dury sounds just right once you've sliced the first piece.

Fruity Peppercorn Cake

This is a deluxe fruit cake - the unlikely combination of peppercorns and fruits take this taste sensation to another level.

Ingredients

250g butter
3 eggs
1 cup brown sugar
½ tsp almond essence
1½ cups self-raising flour
1 cup ground almonds
½ cup roasted hazelnuts, roughly ground
1 cup chopped dates
½ cup chopped dried figs
50g crystallised orange, chopped
50g crystallised ginger, chopped
1 cup currants
1 tin (175g) marinated green peppercorns, drained
½ tsp each cinnamon, ground cardamom and nutmeg
½ cup marmalade
½ cup orange liqueur
¼ cup orange liqueur to brush on cake after cooking

Method

Pre-heat oven to 180°C.

Line 23cm square baking tin with three layers of baking paper.

In large saucepan combine marmalade, orange liqueur, dates, figs, ginger, orange, currants, peppercorns and spices.

Bring gently to the boil, simmer for 10 minutes.

Stir, cover and remove from heat.

Cream butter, sugar and almond essence.

Add eggs one at a time, combine well with each addition.

Stir in flour, ground almonds and hazelnut meal.

Fold in fruit mixture.

Bake in lined square tin on low over 175°C for 2 hours or until skewer tests clean.

Brush with orange liqueur while hot.

Cool in tin.

Remove and wrap in baking paper and foil in airtight container.

The cake can be eaten the next day or brushed with liqueur every week for a couple of months, then eaten.

Make, bake and eat to the very fabulous "Gopher Mambo" by Yma Sumac.

Pear, Fig and Honey Cake
with Orange and Cardamom Glaze

Serve at Rosh Hashana and prepare for a deluge of compliments.

Ingredients

4 pears, peeled, de-seeded and diced
200g dried figs, chopped
1½ cups water
4 eggs
200g melted butter
1 cup caster sugar
100g honey
2 tsp vanilla essence
1 tsp rose water
1 cinnamon stick
2 tsp cinnamon powder
2 cups self-raising flour
1 cup ground hazelnuts
50g sliced almonds

Glaze

Juices from poached pears and figs
6 cardamom pods
Juice and zest of 2 oranges
½ cup sugar
½ cup honey

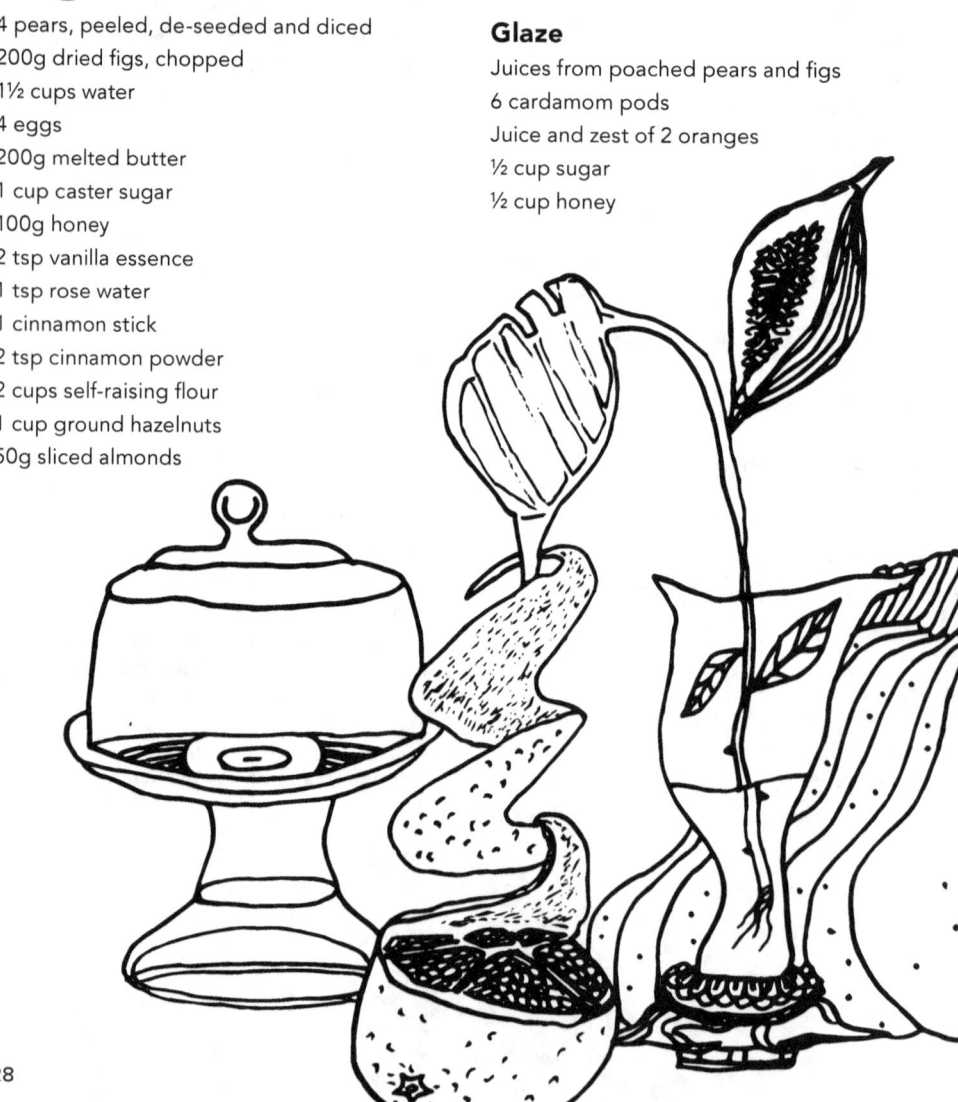

Method

Pre-heat oven to 180°C.

Line 23cm square cake tin with baking paper.

Poach pears and cardamom pods in ½ cup water till pears are soft.

Strain and retain juice and cardamom pods.

Poach chopped figs and cinnamon stick in 1 cup water.

Strain and retain juice and cinnamon stick.

Beat eggs, sugar, honey, rose water, vanilla essence till pale and creamy.

Fold in flour, cinnamon powder and ground hazelnuts.

Fold in melted butter.

Fold in drained pears and figs.

Pour in lined square tin - sprinkle sliced almonds on top.

Bake for around 40-50 minutes or until skewer tests clean.

While cake is cooking prepare glaze.

Pour a third of glaze over cake while hot.

Cool cake in tin.

Serve cake on large square platter with the remainder of the glaze.

Put juices from poached pears and figs, cardamom pods, juice and zest of oranges, sugar and the honey in a pot.

Simmer for around 20 minutes until the glaze is a bit sticky.

Strain the glaze.

Pour ⅓ over the cake when it comes out of the oven.

Pour the remainder of the glaze over the cake just before serving.

If the glaze is too viscous then heat in microwave for 30 seconds and pour over the cake.

Chag Sameach!

Make, bake, eat to the tune of "Mazl" by Karen Feldman and bring on a sweet and happy Jewish New Year. (All songs on the "Mazl" album are glorious. Order Karen Feldman's CD "Mazl Journey Through Yiddish Song" via karenfeldmanmusic.com).

Raspberry, Chocolate and Sour Cream Cake

Whenever I cook this cake, I think of love, the yearning, the passion and the loss. And I think fondly of my old neighbour Carole and all of my tea towels that mysteriously ended up at her house.

Ingredients

3 eggs
1 cup caster sugar
2 cups frozen raspberries
1½ cups self-raising flour
1 cup ground almonds
1 tsp vanilla essence
250g milk chocolate chopped (Whittaker's creamy milk chocolate is best)
150g melted salted butter
1 tub (300ml) sour cream (the Aldi one is very good)

Method

Pre-heat oven to 180°C.

Line 23cm square, 8cm deep cake tin with baking paper (this size tin is preferable but simply adjust cooking times if cake tin size is different).

Use electric beater and mix eggs, sugar and vanilla essence till pale and creamy.

Fold in flour, ground almonds and butter.

Fold in sour cream.

The cake mixture should be yellow and smooth.

Fold in chocolate.

Fold in raspberries (frozen to keep their shape).

Pour into cake tin.

Bake for about 40 minutes or until skewer tests clean and cake is golden.

As this cake bakes and the aroma fills the air, stand for just one moment, inhale deeply and know that you are invincible.

Serve with a pot of Yorkshire Tea.

Make, bake, dance and eat to the beat of "Don't Leave Me This Way" by The Communards.

Matzoh Crack

During Passover, we eat unleavened bread - matzoh - for seven days and we are so over it by then, but add in some chocolate, caramel and almonds and we never want Passover to end.

Ingredients

6 sheets of matzoh
200g butter
1 cup brown sugar
Pinch salt (Maldon Sea Salt Flakes, of course!)
200g dark chocolate, broken into small pieces
100g toasted flaked almonds

Method

Pre-heat oven to 180°C.
Line flat baking tray with baking paper.
Cover the tray with the matzoh sheets - break some to fit, if necessary.
Chop butter, put in a pot with sugar and salt.
Melt and bring to boil slowly for 3 minutes to make caramel.
Pour caramel over the matzoh sheets.
Bake in oven for around 15 minutes. Check every five minutes.
If the caramel gets dark in spots take it out.
Sprinkle dark broken chocolate pieces over the caramel. As it melts, spread evenly with a spatula.
Sprinkle toasted almonds over the chocolate.
Cool in the tray, then break up into uneven pieces and serve.

Play "Sally" by Carmel and have a nice cup of tea or coffee.

Sticky Date Pudding

There's no better date than a sticky one, right?

Ingredients

250g pitted dates, chopped (retain 4 whole dates for garnish on top of cake)
60g butter
2 eggs
1 tsp vanilla
1 tsp bicarbonate of soda
170g caster sugar
170g self-raising flour
300ml water

For the sauce

200g brown sugar
½ cup cream
60g butter

Method

Pre-heat oven to 180°C.
Butter and flour a 24cm loaf tin.
Pour 300ml water over dates in a pan.
Bring to boil, add bicarbonate of soda, stir and set aside.
Cream butter, sugar and vanilla essence.
Add egg, one at a time, beat well with each addition.
Fold in flour.
Stir in date mixture.
Pour into lined loaf tin.
Put the 4 whole dates in a row on top of cake.
Bake at 180°C for around 40 minutes or until skewer tests clean.

For the sauce

Put butter, brown sugar and cream in a pot.
Melt together and stir till blended. Let mixture bubble but not boil.
Simmer for 2-3 minutes.
Remove cake from tin, place on platter.
Pour about a third of the sauce over the cake.
Serve with dollop of cream or good vanilla ice cream and a very strong cup of tea.
This is a comforting cake, and the sauce - well, you could just eat it on its own ...

Take a slice of pudding, pour on the sauce till it floods the plate, make a strong cup of tea and sit by a window looking out, eat slowly and listen to "Shipyards" by Lake Poets.

Acknowledgements

Thank you to my recipe road testers:

Angela Savage and Tash, Karen Glasson, Georgia Cremin and Deb Rechter - your feedback was invaluable!

For all of my friends and family who encouraged me to keep going with Fress with Sless - particularly Dee Wild, Deb Rechter and Karen Glasson.

Curtis Miller for design work.

Emma Cayley for editing.

About

Justine Sless is a Melbourne-based writer and comedian.

Follow on Instagram and Twitter @justinesless

Justine blogs fairly regularly at **Excuse me there are crumbs in my comedy.**

Ruby McDermott is a Melbourne-based illustrator.

www.ingramcontent.com/pod-product-compliance
Lightning Source LLC
Chambersburg PA
CBHW050322010526
44107CB00055B/2353